KINGFISHER
READERS

level
2

P9-DEW-231

Amazing
Animal Senses

Claire Llewellyn

KINGFISHER
NEW YORK

KINGFISHER
LONDON & NEW YORK

Copyright © Kingfisher 2014
Published in the United States by Kingfisher,
175 Fifth Ave., New York, NY 10010
Kingfisher is an imprint of Macmillan Children's Books, London.
All rights reserved.

Distributed in the U.S. and Canada by Macmillan,
175 Fifth Ave., New York, NY 10010

Library of Congress Cataloging-in-Publication data
has been applied for.

Series editor: Thea Feldman
Literacy consultant: Ellie Costa, Bank Street School for Children, New York

ISBN: 978-0-7534-7173-9 (HB)
ISBN: 978-0-7534-7174-6 (PB)

Kingfisher books are available for special promotions
and premiums. For details contact: Special Markets
Department, Macmillan, 175 Fifth Ave., New York, NY 10010.

For more information, please visit
www.kingfisherbooks.com

Printed in China
9 8 7 6 5 4 3 2 1
1TR/0314/WKT/UG/105MA

Picture credits
The Publisher would like to thank the following for permission to reproduce their material. Every care has
been taken to trace copyright holders. However, if there have been unintentional omissions or failure to trace
copyright holders, we apologize and will, if informed, endeavor to make corrections in any future edition.
Top = t; Bottom = b; Center = c; Left = l; Right = r
Cover Shutterstock/mlorenz; Pages 4 Shutterstock/BlueOrange Studio; 5t Photolibrary/Peter Arnold Images;
5b Shutterstock/mypokcik; 6 Shutterstock/Cathy Keifer; 7t Shutterstock/Theodore Mattas; 7b Photolibrary/
Imagebroker; 8–9 Shutterstock/AnetaPics; 10 Shutterstock/Eduard Kyslynskyy/artwork by Sebastian Quigley;
11 Shutterstock/artwork by Sebastian Quigley; 12 Photolibrary/OSF; 13t Photolibrary/Tips Italia;
13b Shutterstock/alle; 14 Frank Lane Picture Agency (FLPA)/Scott Linstead/Minden; 15 Photolibrary/Bridge;
16 Photolibrary/Flirt Collection; 17 Photolibrary/Flirt Collection; 18 Photolibrary/Bios; 19 Photolibrary/Picture
Press; 20 Photolibrary/Bridge; 21 Photolibrary/Bios; 22 Shutterstock/Jason S; 23 Photolibrary/Corbis;
24 FLPA/Angela Hampton; 25 Photolibrary/Imagebroker; 26 FLPA/Dembinsky Press Assoc.; 27 Photolibrary/
Peter Arnold Images; 28 Photolibrary/Imagebroker; 29 FLPA/Tui De Roy/Minden; 30 Corbis/Jean-Bernard
Vernier; 31 Getty/Sandy Huffaker.

Contents

The five senses 4

Animal senses 6

How animals sense things 8

How senses work 10

Take a look! 12

Amazing eyes 14

Now hear this! 16

Amazing ears 18

Taste and smell 20

Amazing tongues and noses 22

That's touching! 24

Amazing feelers 26

Special senses 28

Animal senses can help us 30

Glossary 32

The five senses

Most people and animals have
five senses.

Most people and animals can see, hear, taste, smell, and touch things.

Senses tell us about the world around us!

Animal senses

Animals use their senses to find food, to stay safe, and to find **mates**.

This frog uses its sight
to find and catch a fly.

These deer hear danger nearby,
so they run the other way.

This male
bird sings so
a female mate
can hear him
and find him.

How animals sense things

Every animal, including this dog, has special sense **organs** in its body.

Ears hear sounds.

Eyes see things.

The nose smells things.

Whiskers and skin touch and feel.

The tongue tastes foods.

How senses work

An animal's sense organs and its brain work together.

When this mouse hears a sound,

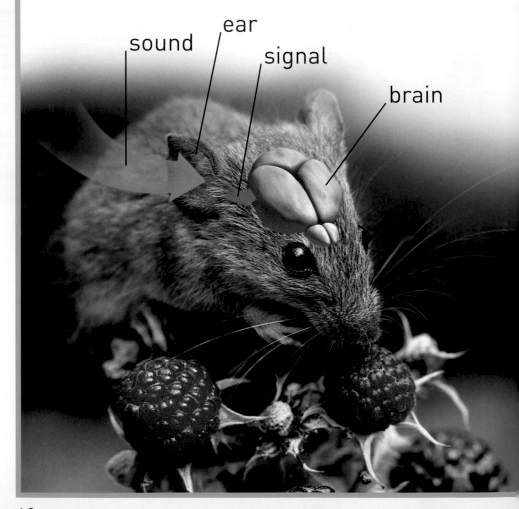

sound   ear   signal   brain

nerves send a signal from the mouse's ear to its brain.

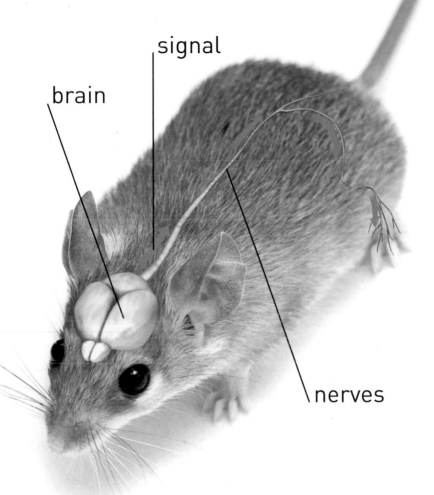

signal

brain

nerves

The brain then sends a signal along the nerves that tells the mouse how to respond to the sound.

Take a look!

An animal uses its sight
to find food, to look out for danger,
and for many other things.

This bee sees bright flowers that
it can land on and find food.

These zebras look around
to make sure no danger is near.

eyes

A snail is low
to the ground,
but its eyes
are not!

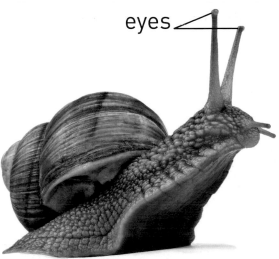

Amazing eyes

An owl has big eyes that face forward.

An owl cannot move its eyes
to the left and right like you can.

It turns its whole head and can see
very far around.

Many insects, like this dragonfly, have huge **compound eyes**, made up of many smaller eyes!

eyes

Now hear this!

An animal uses its hearing
to stay safe, to find its young,
and for many other things.

This hare
turns its
very long ears
to listen for
danger from
all around.

A penguin finds its chick
by listening for the chick's call.

Each chick has its own special call
that a penguin parent can hear,
even with thousands of chicks
calling out in the same place.

Amazing ears

Elephants can hear and call out to each other from about 2.5 miles (4 kilometers) away.

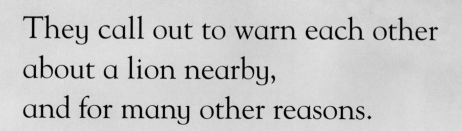

They call out to warn each other about a lion nearby, and for many other reasons.

The squeaks of most **nocturnal** bats
hit objects in the dark
and **echo** back to the bats.

The echo helps a bat to find food
and to avoid bumping into things.

Taste and smell

An animal uses taste to try food, and it uses smell to find things, protect its **territory**, and much more.

A butterfly's taste organs are on its feet, and it stands on a flower to taste it!

This cheetah marks its territory
with strong-smelling **urine**
to tell other cheetahs that
this place is taken!

Amazing tongues and noses

A snake has a nose, but it also smells with its tongue.

It flicks the tongue in and out to smell the air and find food.

A shark's nose helps it find food in the dark sea.

Some sharks can smell even one drop of blood in the water.

That's touching!

An animal uses touch to catch food,
to find its way around,
and for many other things.

A cat uses its whiskers to feel if it
can fit through a small space.

A spider spins
a web to
catch insects.

The spider
feels the
web shake
when an insect
flies into it.

Amazing feelers

Many moles have poor eyesight.

This one uses the pink **tentacles** on its nose to feel its way around and find things, such as food.

The raccoon uses its
very long fingers to feel for fish
and catch them in the water.

Special senses

Every year, some swallows fly thousands of miles to find food and to **breed**.

They have a special sense that works like a **compass** and tells them where to go.

When they are ready to lay eggs, some sea turtles use a special sense to find the same beach where they hatched.

Animal senses can help us

A dog's sense of smell is thousands of times better than a person's.

When people are lost or trapped, a search dog can help find them just by using its nose!

Sea lions have such good sight and hearing that we can train them to find things in the ocean.

Glossary

breed to have babies

compass a tool that helps you find your way

compound eyes eyes made up of many smaller eyes

echo a sound that you hear again, after it bounces off something

mate an animal with whom another animal has babies

nerves wirelike parts of the human body that carry signals to and away from the brain

nocturnal active at night

organs body parts that do specific jobs

tentacles long, stretchy body parts often used to touch things

urine liquid waste that the body gets rid of

territory an area where an animal lives